Introducing Lady Bugley
in flight

****

Clay Pond's first visitor and resident

Dedication:

This book is dedicated to readers who enjoy good storytelling in fiction. The kids will certainly smile when reading it, or when having it read to them.

The Adventure into Nature Begins

The story of Clay Pond is more than a legend; it's an actual account of the lives of every one who ever lived here. Every one was important, and no one was superior to any one else.

We have all of the early records intact, according to our Scribe, Lady Bugley. A meteor landing at the site of an artesian well created the pond. This pond was spring fed as a result and would never run dry.

In the beginning there were many ladybugs from all over that decided to live near this new pond. Lilies began popping up all around the edges; touching the water. Every possible color was seen, even from the trees.

These same trees were home to the ladybugs. But which bug was which was now the big question. They all looked the same, and no one thought to seek out their own name. Instead they were all numbered. The problem was that whichever was number one ruled the pond.

This came to an abrupt end one fateful night as a great storm hit the pond with such ferociousness that lightning destroyed all of the trees around the pond. Sadly, all but one ladybug fell victim to the lightning.

The Fallen

I'll really miss that good old tree
So alive it grew down by the mill
I see her gone as I walk on by
In my mind I see her there still

Proud she was, the tallest of trees
She stood shading all the young there
Her canopy spread over all of them
Her falling had shattered the air

The stump reminds us of this great one
While many came to pay their respect
Some I saw were brushing away tears
While others just came to reflect

The sawmill was good to her that day
She was handled with the utmost care
How worthy she was - a mantle became
Below her a fireplace was there

A mirror was made out of more of her
Many now stare as they look in the glass
A reflection of who she really was
They feel her warm smile as they pass

Crawling out from under a pile of leaves near one of the trees was a young ladybug. The nickname Lady Bugleaf was attached to our only surviving ladybug found alive at the pond. She hated her new name, and insisted everyone call her Lady Bugley instead. It was rather royal sounding. She was the one and only ladybug, after all.

Those who gave her the name Bugleaf were the small birds that would come and go from Clay Pond. It seemed like the best name for her, since she came crawling up out of them, looking like a leaf.

It wouldn't be long before this beautiful pond would attract creatures from far and wide. This would be home to all of them, and our story will show to what extent they lived and interacted with one another.

Could so many varied animals be friends? Some may have been sworn enemies from the beginning. How would that even start to work out here?

There is an ongoing rule at the watering hole.

THE WATERING HOLE

A number of years ago I was asked to be a moderator for a large magazine forum; Writer's Digest. We had no religion forum and many wanted one. I offered to run the site, but wanted to call it a spiritual forum, not "religious forum"; a watering hole where all who live by their many faiths and beliefs could come and share their stories,

and the rest of us would help them hammer out the best piece possible to send to the editor or publisher. In a nutshell, we were all there for one another. The concentration was on the story being told.

THE WATERING HOLE is a place of neutral ground in Africa where all of the animals come together. The animals all respect one another's rights, though they may be predator and prey.

Not everyone is going to agree with the content of ideas here, but the main purpose is to offer a place of neutral ground.

Where Eagles Soar

Our first visitors were a Tortoise and a Snail. But they weren't here to set up camp; instead, our Snail had a hidden agenda.

Tortoise and the Snail

I know why you are here. You thought this was about that turtle and rabbit story. Am I right? This story does start where that tale ended. The turtle was feeling pretty confident after winning the race against the Hare.

Let's all recall that special day for our Turtle

AND THE WINNER IS ...

The Great Race
(The starting gate)
By Don Ford

"Slow and steady always wins it,"
Says the **Tortoise** to the **Hare**.
"So run real fast – you won't offend me.
Keep on bragging, I don't care.

Never will I showcase me.
I've lots to say, but I can wait.
I'm never one to toot my horn.
I will not run out of the gate.

My whole life spent inside this shell.
I'm coming out for this one race.
I'll not say much – I'll keep real quiet

Until that trophy I embrace.

So keep on taunting – laughing at me,
But this one thing do not forget:
I'll run this race in my own pace.
I'll win this one – that you can bet."

The Great Race
(A Hare's Perspective)
By Don Ford

"I know I'll win this race for sure;
Another trophy for my wall.
I've thought about it long and hard,
There's no way I can lose at all.

I can't believe my foe is you.
You think you really have a shot?
A Tortoise isn't known for speed.
I'll take a nap – I brought my cot.

Why don't you simply quit this race?
I've never lost a run so far.
Why don't you pack your *stuff* and go?
This is my turf – I am the star.

So I'll lie back – win easily.
You really are no threat to me.
I've run this route a hundred times
It's in the bag as you will see.

The Turtle Wins
(Final Outcome)
By Don Ford

"At first I thought I would not win.
I didn't stand a chance it's true.
But you were just so self assured.
You were just so full of you.

The whistle blew and I was off.
And when the race it started out,
You laid there smiling in the grass.
You really seemed to have no doubt.

And then you took a little nap.
You lay content upon your cot.
Why would you give me such a lead?
You really thought I had no shot.

I love my shiny golden trophy.
I won the race all fair and square.

I didn't think I stood a chance.
The **Tortoise** truly beat the **Hare**."

Just Not My Day
(**Hare** loss or bad hare day)
By Don Ford

"I've never lost a race before.
This wasn't even close.
I don't know what got in to me.
I guess you could say that I choked.

And then my pride it was to blame,
Just overconfident they say.
I puffed myself all up today.
My great big "I" got in the way.

But next time when I go to race,
I'll keep one thing in mind.
I'll never bring a cot to sleep
I'll stay keyed up – I won't unwind.

I'm just so hyper all the time,
Hopping here and jumping there.
It finally all caught up with me
The **Tortoise** beat me fair and square."

Now seemed like a good time to approach him with a new challenger. Sammy Snail knew how impossible the odds were that he could ever beat the turtle, but Timmy Turtle beat the rabbit with odds that seemed stacked against him as well.

"Excuse me, sir!" The small voice of the snail could hardly be heard as more than a whisper to our turtle. Possibly it was a slight sound in the breeze he was hearing. Then the snail crawled ever so slowly up on the turtle's foot.

"Hey, what's going on down there?" Looking at his left foot, he noticed a small shell creature moving slightly across it. "Get your slimy whatever off of me. Who do you think you are?"

"Just a friend," the snail yelled in the deepest voice he could muster. "I wanted to congratulate you on a job well done. I was rooting for you the whole time."

"Well, thank you. What brings you here to Clay Pond?"

"I know that I am small in everyone's sight, but

I would like to challenge you to a race around this pond."

"You'd stand a better chance, if you raced me across the water to the other side."

"No. I stand a good chance of drowning, as too much water is not good for a snail. I want to race you on the ground."

"Before I say yes to your ridiculous notion, let me ask you a question. Have you ever raced before?"

"No. I haven't, but when I watched you race, it gave me courage, and I know I can do it." Now it was the turtle's turn to laugh, and he did it heartily and with gusto. Once the turtle settled down from all of his rolling on the ground and laughing spell, he approached the snail.

"Look, I'll be honest with you. I beat that rabbit because he brought that cot along to sleep on. I got lucky. I don't even own a cot."

"I'm just asking for the same opportunity that was given to you by the hare. He laughed too, so I'm not offended, nor surprised at your reaction to my request."

"Okay, when do you want this race to begin and where?" The turtle probably thought about the second trophy he could sport when he won hands down. Maybe this might lead to more challenges and more trophies. Lovely ribbons and awards are what he must have been cooking up in his brain.

"I'd like it to start right here where this tiny hill is. I'll climb the hill and you can wait at the bottom until I'm ready at the top. This will give me a decent start. Then the rest of the way we will be on flat ground around the pond."

"I'll even give you a head start. I won't begin until you hit the bottom of the hill."

"I assure you, that won't be necessary."

"The next sound we hear will be the start of the race." The turtle got into position, an once the snail reached the crest of the little knoll, a Canada Goose let out a honk and they were off, sort of. After all, how much action could there be between the two of them?

After what seemed like an eternity, having traveled ten feet, the tortoise glanced back. The snail had been left in the dust. He was nowhere in sight. The turtle kept plodding along as quickly as his short stubby feet would carry him. Did he stop now and then to take a breather? Absolutely not, but he did take the time without stopping to dream about that second trophy on his mantle.

The crowd never saw the start of the race. They were waiting at the other end of the pond. This was too boring for any of them to view. They are the ones with cots to sleep on this time. They gestured to each other to wake them up when it was all over. But all of them fell fast asleep at the finish line.

The turtle could see the end of the race now. It was just up ahead and he could smell victory. Just as he neared the hill and finish line a flock of birds flew over and something fell splat on this head. "Bird dodo, yuck", he screamed as he finished the race across the line. The crowd woke up when he yelled and they began to cheer.

"Hooray, Sammy Snail is the winner."

"Are you all nuts?" Timmy yelled back at them. "I won this race fair and square, and didn't even stop once to rest along the way."

There on top of Timmy's head was our snail perched in all of his glory. He was beaming and was thrilled to receive the award. You see, Sammy wasn't something the birds had dropped, instead he was perched on the hill and jumped down at the right moment, leaning just far enough forward to garner the win. He literally won by an antenna.

Our tortoise had nothing to say as he

sauntered off into the pond to drown his sorrows. He chose to keep his dignity in tact, and not seem like a sore loser, like our rabbit earlier.

Here is the snail picture that my 10 year old, Erin, did for me. She knew I was doing pictures and poems at the time, and I needed a snail picture for a snail poem I had written. She said, "Dad, I can be your artist." And when she produced this from a paint program, I was thrilled.

"Yes you can be my artist," I said.

The Snail : To Be or Should it Be?

A snail, it has no purpose,
You hear 'um haw and hem.
But scientists and naturalists
Beg to differ with them.

The tests are not conclusive.
The verdict is still out.
There has to be a reason,
These men you hear them shout.

The research is progressing
Their fate is in good hands.
They view the creature out of house,
Like a mini whale on land.

Their shell could use a study
Like the armor of a knight.
A house that fits them like a glove,
And hides them out of sight

Let rain come down in peltings
The snail returns to home and castle
And wind - its icy blast - come too.
But safely does our snail sleep well,

And someday we will know the truth;
What brings us to discussing.
Why are these snails here at all?
Why is there so much fussing?

Hit and Miss

Summer was long gone. Winter was not far away. The leaves on most of the trees had blown off by now, only the evergreens were left wearing their winter coats. The nights seemed longer and colder. Blustery winds swept over the land. The sounds of winter had begun to ring through the forest. The scents of pine, spruce, and even fir trees, were strong in the air.

Many v-shaped formations were headed across the sky. The visiting birds of summer had once again gathered together and were preparing to leave for warmer places.

Animals such as skunks, rabbits, and squirrels were getting ready to hibernate for the winter. Food and supplies were being stockpiled for the long, cold months ahead. Preparation for the rigors of winter was the current business.

In the valley there was a family of foxes living in a nice warm cave. They were not alone there; other animals were also taking shelter in this giant opening in the rocks. Mr. Bear had settled in and had gone to sleep, at the back of the cave. A pair of squirrels was scampering about, carrying nuts and acorns in their cheeks. Every creature was preparing for a long, hard winter.

The fox family had grown considerably and it was time for some of the youngsters to launch out and establish their own families in other areas of the country. The food scarcity in the immediate area prompted one young fox to decide to leave home. He headed off through the mouth of the cave, trying not to look back as the others saw him off.

I'm sure he wondered at the time if he would ever see his family members again. His coat was full by now, and would certainly keep him warm through the coming winter. Snow would be upon them all soon. Our young Mr. Fox would find his own special shelter when he arrived at his destination.

He would have to find another cave or suitable cavity in a tree or the ground as lodgings for the winter. Food would be the next item on the agenda. He had learned how to hunt prey from his parents. Now he would have to learn to employ his skills for the purpose of securing his own meals. This was an anxious time for any young fox.

It's difficult being alone in the world. Mr. Fox had plenty of friends in the cave along with his family, but he had made the decision to lead his own life. There was no turning back now. He wanted to start his own family in a new territory, so he began his long journey to a new pond, where he had heard that the duck population was huge. Just thinking about it made his mouth water.

Clay Pond was a different sort of a place. The creatures there all looked out for each other. When trouble came, they alerted one another. Our fox headed into this new area in the hope of making new friends, and finding plenty of morsels to eat.

As a young fox, he found that he had few friends, because of being the predator that he had to be at times. Yes, it was true that he was sly, but this was what got him through life. Please don't think of him as being dishonest, after all, every animal has got to eat. He saw himself as being clever, rather than crafty, even if he did have to break a few rules now and then.

The next few weeks proved to be lean ones for Mr. Fox Junior. He had no luck hunting for a good meal. Ducks were his preferred food. He couldn't get enough of them. But where were they all? Had they forgotten that there was a wonderful pond here for their swimming pleasure?

The weather had been good for several weeks, but even if it rained, the ducks should still come.

Don't they actually love rain as long as they aren't flying in it? Pools of water had formed along the roadsides. Surely that should be a welcome sight for ducks?

A fox has only so much patience and his was wearing thin. He suddenly felt abandoned. Maybe a warning had gone out among the pond friends that the fox was hiding in wait for the ducks. How much longer could our youthful fox wait before heading for greener pastures and other ponds?

Then, one morning, the young fox could not believe his luck. The day before there had been no sign of any ducks on the water. Now suddenly, the pond seemed like a convention. Hundreds of the tasty fowl had landed quite near him.

Mr. Fox could now look forward to a day of abundance. He wouldn't have to sneak up on his dinner. He could simply charge the enormous flock of birds, and easily grab a duck and run. It had been too long since he had had such a wonderful opportunity. The smell of duck was simply intoxicating. He pinched himself to be sure it wasn't all a dream. He hadn't eaten for a long time, but finally the waiting was over.

From twenty feet away he spotted a beauty. With a choice of so many, why not grab the best and tastiest looking one? This was going to be too easy for our fox. So, setting his feet into running mode, he dove into a pile of ducks and retrieved his prize. The thunderous swell of the flapping of wings echoed through the air as our fox retreated with his chosen morsel firmly in his grasp. Now to enjoy his long anticipated meal.

Young Mr. Fox took his first real bite of the yummy looking duck. Such a surprised look came over his face as he came close to breaking his jaw. His meal was too stiff to eat. Had he selected a duck that was dead? Had rigor mortis set in so soon?

No! The prettiest duck on the water that day was a decoy.

It was the impostor who had drawn all the other ducks to the pond, and at the same time, had saved the lives of all the other living birds. From that day forward, the young fox determined that he would never be taken in by beauty alone, the skin-deep nature of which had proved to be such a disappointment.

THE LONE DRAGONFLY

(A Sequel to Hit and Miss) By Don Ford

After his successful, but unrewarding, capture of the Decoy Duck, all that young Mr. Fox had to look forward to was yet another hungry day on his own in the apparently food-less wilderness in which he had himself chosen to live. Well, maybe that's not quite the way that things were, but after such a disappointment the day before, our hero was depressed and inclined to think the worst of his prospects.

Nevertheless, he thought that perhaps today would be a better day to try his luck at the pond. Our fox was still very hungry. A thought occurred to him, as a last resort he would have only the tall grasses to eat. He did not look forward to that prospect.

Moving slowly in the direction of the pond, this time lying on his stomach and doing an awkward crawl, he made his way toward the water where the flight of duck had resettled and where they had spent the night.

Before reaching the pond, he encountered another creature that was also crawling on its belly. This slithering approach just has to be the answer, the fox thought, as he continued moving in the same manner. The other creature obviously knew what it was doing, since it looked as if it must have been doing things this way for ages.

Face to face with a large snake, our youngster had to make a decision. He could perhaps have snake for dinner today instead of duck, he thought. He had never eaten snake before, nor had he ever heard of a family member having done this, but desperate times call for desperate measures!

The snake must have suddenly realized the danger it was facing and slithered off, out of reach, into a hole in the rocks. The fox was upset. This was one time when he should not have stopped to think before going into action; he should have just gone ahead and done what he had to do. Now the waiting for food would continue.

Having, in the past, heard so many stories about Clay Pond, he wondered what had happened to the supposedly easy life around there. At one time this place had been a busy hub brimming with all sorts of life around its edges or swimming in its water.

Our fox wondered if even one of the stories of the past regarding this place was true. His grandfather was known to be a great storyteller. Even older foxes had come to hear him spin his yarns back in the home den. Were all his stories just fiction and fox lore, not firmly based on truth or reality?

The most impressive tale he remembered his grandfather telling was about the Great Swarm of black flies that travel in huge flying communities. Their goal was simple, to drain the lifeblood out of their intended victim. His Grandfather claimed that he told this story from first-hand knowledge and experience, for he had once been in danger of being their next victim.

The way the story went, Grandfather was sitting near the south end of Clay Pond, when the attack took place. To the east of him was this swarm of flying insects. They looked like a huge dark spot in the sky until they got close. Then he could see that each and every one of them was heading his way.

He ran, but he didn't stand a chance. They were all over him like a bad rash. Fortunately, he had not been the only one with an eye on the horde of insects. From another corner of the pond came help. If the Black Flies were relentless, the new flyer was on a mission too!

Enter Mr. Dragonfly! As he flew in and out among the insects he was gulping them down

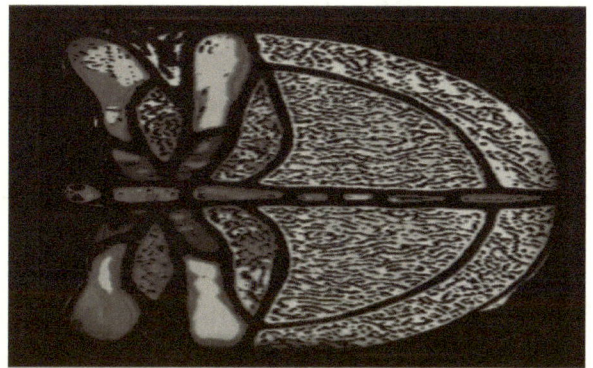

by the hundreds. Within minutes every one of the pests had been eaten. Put together one amazing dragonfly, hundreds of black flies, and the old fox's problems were a thing of the past and the stuff that legends were made of.

Remembering these old stories took our young fox's mind off his stomach momentarily, but when you're hungry, you're just plain hungry, and no amount of stories can soothe the pain of an empty belly. Mr. Fox still had to find something to eat. Though the problem was an urgent one, in such conditions it is only too easy to become careless and make mistakes, so he resolved to be extra cautious this time as he drew nearer to the pond.

Trouble was indeed closer than he imagined. He noticed, tucked away in a duck blind, two hunters armed with rifles. Men with guns were sometimes careless and needed to be watched. Our young fox promptly decided that he would lie low until they left. Then he could safely go on to the pond to resume his own search for food.

The hours went by, but still the humans sat there. Then suddenly, the guns went off. The flock of ducks took off, leaving two of their kind floating, dead, in the water. On the way to retrieve their victims, the two hunters unexpectedly found themselves face to face with the local game warden.

"These ducks were shot out of season! I will need to see your identification papers."

The men walked off with sad faces and the prospect of a hefty fine. The warden finished his paperwork and then he left also.

Oh, the two ducks? That's where young Mr. Fox comes in. He could take a break from having to look for food now. Thanks to the hunters, and the game warden, dinner had just been served!

Other Kid readings

by Don G. Ford

Life is all about variety, and nowhere is that truer than in the animal kingdom. There are different kinds of dogs, horses, fish, rabbits; you name it.

This book will take you into the lives of many of those animals. If you didn't care before, or know that you should, remember that many of these creatures are vanishing from off the Earth.

(FULL COLOR) https:// www.createspace.com/ 4307772

The purpose of this compilation of short stories, vignettes, and poems is to turn a few smiles right side up. You'll run into spiders, ghosts and even the little "Fly on the Wall". It's all in fun and for everyone's reading pleasure. If you have your boots on, jump right in. Every chapter here is a...

Publication Date: March 28, 2013

www.createspace.com/4203459

https://www.createspace.com/4504489

Overview Friends come in all sizes, colors, and species. Children and those young at heart will enjoy this display of simple fun as we look into the lives of two very different characters, who we find in the end are not so different. This tale is really for the kid in all of us. A fun loving, carefree, and learning experience for children today.

MORE STORIES

Chilly The Very Warm-Blooded Polar Bear

Raising Hope

Mirrored Self

Tree with the Money on it

Furry Business

Floyd the Dog Story Book Commemorative

CONNECT THE DOTS

Clay Pond - Lady Fugley

Clay Pond and Other Fish Tails

Clay Pond - We All Love Lacy

Clay Pond - What is a Yoodie?

FROM DON'S LIBRARY

www.ingramcontent.com/pod-product-compliance
Lightning Source LLC
Chambersburg PA
CBHW030547290526
45786CB00004B/1901